Anonymous

Ceremonies at the Dedication of the Soldiers' Monument in Concord, Mass

Anonymous

Ceremonies at the Dedication of the Soldiers' Monument in Concord, Mass

ISBN/EAN: 9783337307158

Printed in Europe, USA, Canada, Australia, Japan

Cover: Foto ©ninafisch / pixelio.de

More available books at **www.hansebooks.com**

CEREMONIES

AT

THE DEDICATION

OF THE

SOLDIERS' MONUMENT,

IN

CONCORD, MASS.

—◆—

CONCORD:
PRINTED BY BENJAMIN TOLMAN.
1867.

THE MONUMENT.

The Town of Concord, true to the principles which found voice and action in the war of the Revolution, was among the first in the State to respond to the call to arms of President Lincoln.

Its military company left the town to take part in the defence of the national capital, on the 19th of April, 1861; and from that time until the war closed it had, almost without intermission, one company, and for a portion of the period, two in the field, whose members were recruited mostly within its boundaries and from among its citizens.

As a natural consequence, it was often called upon during the bloody struggle to mourn the loss of some one of the number, who had gone forth to the fight; and, soon after the war was over. it sought some means of showing its high appreciation of its heroic dead.

The first definite action was taken by the town at the town-meeting on March 19th, 1866, when a Com-

mittee of the citizens, twenty-five in number, was chosen, and a sum of money appropriated to erect such a testimonial as they might think proper.

This Committee immediately came together, and, having decided upon a site in the square in front of the Town-House, and selected an appropriate design for a Monument, proceeded at once with the work.

The Monument was completed about the first of April, 1867, and a Committee was appointed to make arrangements for fitting ceremonies of dedication, which took place on the 19th of April, the 92nd anniversary of the first battle of the Revolution, fought in this town in 1775.

The weather, on the day of dedication, was most propitious; and a large number of the citizens of the town, with invited guests and old residents of the place, formed in procession under the escort of the military company, and marched to the old battle-ground and around its Monument, and from thence to the front of the Town-House, where the exercises took place, the Hon. John S. Keyes acting as President of the Day, who made the following

OPENING ADDRESS.

Friends and Fellow-Citizens:

Our ancestors were patriotic. In the Indian wars — in the Revolution — in the war of 1812 — they did their duty, and they did it well. This is the past. Of the present you need not be told, — you all know the services and the sacrifices of the war of the Rebellion.

In the cares and labors that follow war, we do not forget our heroic dead. Mindful of their duties, we have the right to perpetuate their record.

But we do this not in boast. It is in remembrance; not in ostentation. Our fathers erected a monument "on the spot where the first of the enemy fell, in the war of that revolution which gave independence to these United States." The vanquished, not the victors, sleep in its quiet shade. This is Concord. This is Peace.

To-day we dedicate another shaft "to the brave men" who were "faithful unto death." Their names and their memories we meet to consecrate. Their lives, their deeds, their deaths, we enshrine. To them belongs this occasion. Theirs, not ours, are its honors. Theirs were the toils, the hardships, the sufferings. Ours are the fruits of their victories.

Gratefully, kindly, honorably, we would commemorate their example. In our hearts we cherish their

memory. On yonder stone we grave their record. The gratitude, the remembrance, the affection will endure while we live, and the graven record shall tell of it and them

"When, like our sires, our sons are gone."

PRAYER.

By Rev. Mr. Reynolds.

Almighty God! Thou who wast the God of our fathers amid the struggles and dangers of the past; Thou who hast been the God and Gracious Father of their children, in the mighty conflicts of the present; we lift our hearts to Thee in prayer. We beseech Thee to send Thy grace into our hearts, that they may be in harmony with the thoughts, the memories and the lessons of this hour.

Giver of all good gifts! We rejoice in this bright and beautiful day, which lifts our hearts to Thee in filial trust; when all Thy works speak of that presence which blesses and guards every one of Thy children. With gratitude we gather in this blessed time of peace, which has succeeded the time of war and carnage; and we thank Thee that its tranquil hours are made more sacred and precious by the remembrance that the heroism and fidelity of those who sealed their loyalty even by their own blood, have established the more perfect reign of justice and liberty in the land. Fill our breasts with unfeigned thankfulness, that when the season of trial came — when evil counsels sought to overthrow that fabric of law and liberty which our fathers had bequeathed to us — brave and faithful

men were found; that they came forth from all our peaceful homes, our husbands and brothers, our fathers and sons, by their courage and patience to sustain and perpetuate the privileges which had been handed down to us. Help us to rejoice as we ought in the pure and generous sentiments which inspired them, and in the spiritual nobility with which our institutions of knowledge and religion had filled their souls.

O Thou, who in Thine infinite goodness dost direct and bless all just counsels; we acknowledge that it was Thy wisdom, which in the fulness of time raised up brave leaders, skilful generals, and rulers who feared God and loved justice, so to direct the courage and patience of our soldiers that treason and slavery might be destroyed, and the nation born into a new life of freedom and righteousness. And we bless Thy great and holy name that good men did not struggle in vain; that they did not suffer and die in vain; that not one tear has been shed, that not one place has been made vacant in our homes, that not one brave life has ended on battle-field or in hospital, or in cruel prison-house, without helping Thy holy kingdom to come on the earth.

Most Merciful Father! Who by Thy spirit canst direct the thoughts of men, dispose our minds to receive the hallowing influences of this hour. As we rear a Monument to the memory of those who have

suffered and given their lives for us, bless, we pray Thee, our offering. Fill our hearts with affectionate memories and deep and tender gratitude, so that the silent stone, which commemorates their virtues and sacrifices, may forevermore quicken in us a noble and patriotic life. Help us to treasure up the example of our heroic dead, that it may deepen our sense of responsibility, and hallow our loyal and faithful purposes. In all the future may the things which are true, the things which make for human freedom and the things which are for the upbuilding and blessing of mankind, have a profounder power over us because of these brave and truehearted men.

Great Ruler of Worlds! We pour forth our petition for our common country. We pray for that country, which our fathers dedicated to Christian faith and righteousness, and which has been baptized anew to freedom and truth in the blood of those who have died for it. We pray that we may be a people whose God is the Lord; that our nation may be built up, not on material prosperity alone; that it may be strong, not only in broad boundaries and in rich possessions, but strong through faith in Thee, strong in loyalty to the truth and strong in the everlasting principles of right which govern its life; that those who are called to legislate may enact laws in the fear of God and in the love of justice; that those who rule

over us may execute those laws with fidelity and impartiality; that our citizens may seek to do Thy will; so that we shall become a people who in all their ways revere and serve God.

Heavenly Father! Bless the praises, the prayers and the memories of this hour. May our life henceforth seem more sacred on account of them. Feeling how costly a sacrifice has been offered up for us, may we go forth from the thoughts of this time to a better fulfilment of all the duties which belong to us as citizens of a great and free country, as immortal beings and as Thy children.

In memory of those who are dear to us, of those who went forth from our homes, who were bone of our bone and flesh of our flesh, who were bound to us by all sweet and friendly ties, we have reared this Monument. Consecrate it, O our Father, in our hearts! May it stand evermore, to remind us of duty, and to make us more loyal, more heroic and more faithful to Thee. We ask it, Father, in the name of Jesus Christ, our Lord. Amen.

ODE.

By George B. Bartlett.

(Air: Auld Lang Syne.*)*

Beneath the shadow of the elm, where ninety years ago
Old Concord's rustic heroes met to face a foreign foe,
We come to consecrate this Stone to heroes of to-day,
Who perished in a holy cause as gallantly as they.

The patriot preacher's bugle-call, that April morning knew,
Still lingers in the silver tones of him who speaks to you;
As on their former muster-ground called by its notes again,
Those ancient heroes seem to greet brave Prescott and his men.

And as each soldier-saint appears to answer to his name,
Not one has dimmed the lustre of its old, unconquered fame;
They, too, have left their peaceful homes for scenes of bloody strife,
And death has turned to hallowed ground the fields they tilled in life.

The Bronze and Stone we proudly rear must surely pass away,
But deathless lives of fallen braves can never know decay;
For, freed from stain of slavery, our re-united land —
The soldiers' truest monument — shall ever firmly stand.

REPORT

OF THE

MONUMENT COMMITTEE,

BY E. R. HOAR, CHAIRMAN.

The Committee chosen by the town a year ago, to erect a Monument to our soldiers who died in the war of the Rebellion, have performed the duty assigned to them, and to-day report to the inhabitants of Concord the finished work. The means placed at their disposal were the town appropriations, of $4,500, and the gift by Mr. James B. Brown, of $100.

The cost of the Monument has been —

For the Architect's Plan and Superintendence,	$150 00
For the Stone-Work and Foundation,	3,500 00
For the two Bronze Tablets,	600 00
For a Plan of the Ground and Temporary Fence,	54 12
Amounting in the whole to	$4,304 12
And leaving toward the Grading of the Grounds and their Permanent Enclosure an unexpended balance of	$295 88

There was, as might be expected, some difference of opinion in regard to the best site for the Monument; but that which was selected was the preference of a very large majority of the Committee, and, so far as they could ascertain, was approved by the general sentiment of the town. The Monument is a *cenotaph*, and

marks no place of burial; so that it need not seek its place in a cemetery. It commemorates a great public service; is the offering of public gratitude; and claims the most public, conspicuous, and honorable position.

For a design, we sought the assistance of an architect eminent for taste and skill, Mr. Hammatt Billings, of Boston. He has furnished one which seems to us symmetrical in its proportions, graceful in outline, producing an effect both elegant and massive; "Latiore initio tenuem in ambitum metae modo exsurgens."

The Monument rests on a solid foundation, and is built of durable and indestructible material. The contractors for building it were Messrs. Abijah and Thomas Hollis, of Concord, New Hampshire, who have done their work thoroughly and well. The castings were made by Messrs. Henry L. Hooper & Co., of Boston, and are good specimens of the excellence of their workmanship. The simple and unpretending beauty of the whole structure deserves and must receive an increasing public favor. For a community so small and of so little wealth, it may seem, in these days of high prices and burdensome taxation, that we have expended a large sum. But as with the "box of ointment, very precious," it is not "waste" to bring a costly tribute of gratitude and love.

A stone, taken from the abutment of the Old North Bridge and placed at the foundation of this Monument,

is a fitting memorial of the relation of the 19th of April, 1775, to the 19th of April, 1861; and Buttrick, and Davis, and Hosmer admit to their fellowship the men who in their turn have offered their lives for their country, for freedom and the rights of mankind.

The inscription on one of the tablets of bronze declares that

THE
TOWN OF CONCORD
BUILDS THIS MONUMENT
IN HONOR OF
THE BRAVE MEN
WHOSE NAMES IT BEARS:
AND RECORDS
WITH GRATEFUL PRIDE,
THAT THEY FOUND HERE
A BIRTHPLACE, HOME OR GRAVE.
1866.

The lettered stones on the sides bear the date

1861
TO
1865.

on one side; the words

FAITHFUL
UNTO
DEATH.

on the other.

The inscription on the other tablet is the single sentence

THEY DIED FOR THEIR COUNTRY IN THE
WAR OF THE REBELLION.

with the thirty-two names:

32nd Regiment, M. V.

Col. GEORGE L. PRESCOTT,
Serg't CHARLES APPLETON,
Corp. WILLIAM J. DAMON,
FRANCIS BUTTRICK.
BARNEY CLARK.
GEORGE B. ERSKINE,
JONAS E. MELVIN.

2nd Regiment, M. V.
THOMAS CAREY.

9th Regiment, M. V.
MARTIN LYNCH.

16th Regiment, M. V.
HERMAN FLINT.

20th Regiment, M. V.
EDWARD GARRITY, | JOHN McDONOUGH.

29th Regiment, M. V.
Lieut. EZRA RIPLEY.

40th Regiment, M. V.
GEORGE J. CARR, | CHARLES P. HANNAFORD,
ALONZO H. MUNROE.

47th Regiment, M. V.
Serg't FRANK M. GREGORY, | Corp. E. H. KINGSBURY,
OLIVER M. RICHARDS.

53d Regiment, M. V.
CHARLES W. STUART.

56th Regiment, M. V.
MICHAEL MURRAY.

59th Regiment, M. V.
RICHARD R. CLARK, | GEORGE POLAND,
HENRY SMITH.

1st Regiment Mass. H. A.
PAUL A. DUDLEY, JOHN H. MELVIN,
ASA H. MELVIN, SAMUEL MELVIN,
CHARLES NEALEY.

1st Regiment Mass. Cavalry.
THOMAS DOYLE.

1st Regiment Michigan Vols.
ALDEN BUTTRICK.

17th Regiment Ohio Vols.
CHARLES H. WRIGHT.

Of these thirty-two men, twenty-four lived in Concord at the time of their enlistment, and formed a part of the quota of the town. Four, who belonged to Concord, entered the service from other places. Two, natives of the town, and who had grown up to manhood among us, had found homes elsewhere, but were brought back to their birthplace for burial. One, descended through a long line of Concord ministers from Peter Bulkeley, the first minister of the town and the leader in its settlement, has come to sleep with his fathers. And the other, born and educated in sight of the Old North Bridge, where his great-grandfather led his neighbors in the first conflict of the Revolution, is too thoroughly identified with Concord in name and lineage to need an explanation of his claim to a place on our roll of honor. All of them have found here a birthplace, home or grave.

These names represent all classes and conditions of life which our little community contains. Twenty-seven of them were Americans by birth; five, Americans by choice. There are found on the list members of our oldest families, who have held these farms and tilled these fields for more than two hundred years; and, mingled with theirs, in honor as in fate, the names of adopted citizens, of whose devotion to the great country which welcomed them to its privileges, opportunities and duties, it is enough to say, that they died for it. As the names are read, we remember the delicate boy who gave up ease and comfort and wealth and friends, a happy home and the hopes of a bright future, to sink under the hardships, exposures and fatigues of a private soldier. And we do not forget the child of poverty, temptation and neglect, thrown upon the world with all the passions and appetites of unregulated youth; and think with pity and tenderness that he atoned for the errors of a short life by faithful service and an honorable death.

"They died for their country!" There is no fame so spotless that it does not gain new lustre from that luminous record! No life so humble or so worthless that it is not dignified and ennobled by that epitaph! The altar sanctifies the gift. "Greater love hath no man than this, that a man lay down his life for his friends."

How poor is all that we can say of them compared with what they have done for us! We place their names upon the monument, and that is all. Yet how few of us will attain such enduring memory, or leave behind us such a permanent influence. It is something, while this generation lasts, that these names, which recall to wives and children and fathers and mothers the costly sacrifice of their households, will be preserved and cherished; that kindred and friends will find consolation in this public recognition, and in the assurance that, through a long future, they are to be held in undying remembrance and honor. And more than this is true. This war of the Rebellion was a war of the people, for the people. The ties that connected the men who went to the war with the communities to which they belonged, were never severed for a moment; and nothing cheered the heart and nerved the arm of the soldier so much as the ever-present idea of what would be thought and said of him at home. They could face death, but they hoped and believed that they would not be forgotten. To the bravest of them it was not a matter of indifference

> "Whether praise of him should walk the earth
> Forever, and to noble deeds give birth,
> Or he must fall, to sleep without his fame,
> And leave a dead, unprofitable name."

An affecting incident of the war will illustrate this.

On Monday, Nov. 30th, 1863, an attack on the enemy's lines at Mine Run was ordered by Gen. Meade, and countermanded at the last moment by Gen. Warren, on his own responsibility, when he saw that it was desperate. The historian of the Army of the Potomac tells us: "His verdict was that of his soldiers, — a verdict pronounced, not in spoken words, but in a circumstance more potent than words, and full of a touching pathos. Recognizing that the task before them was of the character of a forlorn-hope, knowing well that no man could here count on escaping death, the soldiers, without sign of shrinking from the sacrifice, were seen quietly pinning on the breast of their blouses of blue, slips of paper on which each had written *his name*."

Their names shall live. They shall teach those who come after us lessons of patriotism and courage. The children of the village shall spell them out, and learn them by heart. The young men shall be trained by them in the shining ways of disinterested virtue; and the cowardly and selfish shall always feel their silent rebuke. Let them stand forever upon the tablet to testify for us, that " a living dog is" *not* "better than a dead lion."

We cannot give in detail the story of the fallen, though there are hearts which throb with peculiar emotion as each is mentioned. There are the names

of three brothers, giving to one family a sad distinction. Another family, which also gave three brothers to the war, finds the name of one upon the list which has been read to you, and rejoices with us that two were spared. Two names recall the unutterable horrors of Andersonville, and will never suffer us to forget that our armies conquered barbarism as well as treason.

To this solemn roll-call there comes a response from the trenches of Petersburg, from Carolina and Mississippi, from Maryland and Tennessee, from the Wilderness, from Gettysburg and Antietam. In the shadowy procession which we invoke are the forms of those who fell gloriously in battle; of the victims of accident, disease and exhaustion; and of those who perished by cruelties which made death welcome. Some have been borne to their last resting-place in the village graveyard, followed by the prayers and tears and reverent sorrow of neighbors and kindred; and to some, who sleep where they fell, we are paying the first funeral honors in the solemnities of this day.

And first of all, in rightful place as in military rank, comes the name which it is not invidious to single out for special and peculiar commemoration to-day, the name of George L. Prescott. The gigantic scale on which the war was waged, with generals by the hundred and colonels by the thousand, excludes from a national reputation all but the few who held the most conspicuous

posts. Yet among the myriads of the brave and noble, each State, and city, and town may cherish the fame of its own hero; — and *he* was ours.

Born of the sturdy stock of the yeomanry of Middlesex, educated in our common schools, he was left at an early age the pride and hope of a widowed mother, and grew up in Concord under the influences of the church and the Sunday-school, the lyceum, the library, the town-meeting and the battle-ground. With a vigorous frame, and a form of manly beauty, he was self-reliant, frank, truthful, generous and modest. From a boy he had played at soldiering in the Concord Artillery, and had risen to be its ornamental lieutenant, — a noticeable figure on parade and at military balls. He was a fine specimen of the product of our New England country towns. He had no restless ambition, urging him to seek for personal distinction; no love of battle or of victory. His tastes were all peaceful, social, friendly. He had a pleasant home and a contented spirit; and, popular among his townsmen and neighbors, to whom his cordial greeting and readiness for all the little offices of kindness were so familiar, he might well have looked forward to a long and tranquil and happy life. But the day of trial came. When the wise forethought of Gov. Andrew took the precaution to ascertain how many of the militia of Massachusetts would hold themselves ready to attend the call of the

country whenever it should be made, he had answered,
with the rest, that he would go. And when that call
was heard, on the morning of the 19th of April, he left
his home,—in sight of that memorable spot where the
deeds of our fathers made the day immortal,—and went
forth to redeem his pledge. Some of us may now remember with remorseful sadness, that, in the excite-
ments of that memorable day, we were impatient even
of the pleadings of domestic love, which presaged too
truly the seriousness of the decision which he was called
to make. But with the heart of a boy he had the soul
of a man. The love of justice, freedom, country, pos-
sessed it. He chose the path of duty, of honor, of
patriotism, of glory; alas! that it led so swiftly to the
grave. An only son, an only brother, a husband and a
father, with no sufficient provision made for his wife
and children, he had everything to make life dear and
desirable, and to require others to hesitate for him, if
he did not hesitate for himself. But deeply as he must
have felt the pang which his departure gave to those
most dear to him, it would seem that a serene and satisfied joy would have impressed itself on his face in
death, as that lofty utterance of loving lips, from the
profoundest depths of a loving heart, was spoken over
his coffin: "Better *so*, than that he should not have
gone."

It is unquestionably to his spirit and example that it was due, that our town was enabled to respond to the call of the President, by sending an organized company to the defence of the national capital on the 19th of April, 1861. He said in this hall, on that morning, "I intend to go, if I go alone." And from the hour when, as lieutenant commanding, he mustered his men on this floor, to that terrible month of battles, in Grant's advance on Richmond in 1864, when, colonel of his regiment, and for nineteen successive days under fire, the fatal bullet pierced his breast, he continued the same resolute, patient, modest, intrepid soldier and man. On the disastrous day of Bull Run, he came back alone, the last of his company to leave the field. His instinctive sympathies taught him from the outset what many higher in command were so slow and so late to learn, that it is the first duty of an officer to take care of his men as much as to lead them. His character developed new and larger proportions, with new duties and larger responsibilities.

Our whole population was moved, as never before, at his funeral. His face looks down from that wall upon your public meetings, and his sweet and gracious memory gives a new glory to this April holiday. There is no benefactor like him who leaves to us the record of a pure life, and a great example. To the grave where he lies let his townsmen and strangers turn with rev-

erent feet; and let maidens strew upon it garlands and flowers! "Bring lilies with full hands," and myrtle and laurel, and the unfading amaranth!

Fellow-citizens of Concord: The martyrs whom we honor were of the average population of the town, yet so many were found "faithful unto death." The occasion belongs to the dead, and you have elsewhere expressed your gratitude to the living. But the surviving soldiers, the comrades of the fallen, will find in these solemnities your estimate of their own services.

The Monument which we consecrate to-day establishes a new bond of union among the inhabitants of this town. It is a new incentive to duty, patriotism and fidelity. It speaks to you of public spirit, of manly virtue, of something higher than life, — of immortality. As the seasons come and go, in summer's heat and winter's storms, catching the first beams of the morning, and reflecting the last rays of the setting sun, in the full blaze of noon, and under the silent stars of midnight, this structure will stand, immovable, enduring, our witness before heaven. While we cherish in our hearts the cause for which these soldiers gave their lives, the cause of justice, freedom and equal rights, its presence will be grateful and honorable to us. But if ever the time shall come when treason or tyranny shall here find apologists or defenders, or the hearts of men shall fail them for fear in the hour of their

country's need, these stones will speak the shame of the living, though they will stand a monument of glory to the illustrious dead.

E. R. HOAR,
RICHARD BARRETT,   GEORGE KEYES,
GEORGE M. BROOKS,   JOHN S. KEYES,
DAVID BUTTRICK,   G. W. LAURIAT,
H. H. BUTTRICK,   S. LOVEJOY,
J. M. CHENEY,   SAMPSON MASON,
E. C. DAMON,   G. REYNOLDS,
LORENZO EATON,   JULIUS M. SMITH,
R. W. EMERSON,   S. STAPLES,
A. G. FAY,   N. B. STOW,
J. P. GEORGE,   L. A. SURETTE,
A. J. HARLOW,   EDWIN WHEELER,
GEORGE HEYWOOD,   ALBERT E. WOOD,

Monument Committee.

ADDRESS,
BY R. W. EMERSON.

ADDRESS.

Fellow-Citizens :

The day is in Concord doubly our calendar day, as being the anniversary of the invasion of the town by the British troops in 1775 ; and of the departure of the company of volunteers for Washington, in 1861. We are all pretty well aware that the facts which make to us the interest of this day are in a great degree personal and local here; that every other town and city has its own heroes and memorial days, and that we can hardly expect a wide sympathy for the names and anecdotes which we delight to record. We are glad and proud that we have no monopoly of merit. We are thankful that other towns and cities are as rich ; that the heroes of old and of recent date, who made and kept America free and united, were not rare or solitary growths, but sporadic over vast tracts of the Republic. Yet, as it is a piece of nature and the common sense that the throbbing chord that holds us to our kindred, our friends and our town, is not to be denied or resisted, — no matter how frivolous or unphilosophical its pulses, — we shall cling affectionately to our houses, our river and pastures, and believe that our visitors will pardon us if we take the privilege of talking freely about our nearest

neighbors as in a family party; — well assured, meantime, that the virtues we are met to honor were directed on aims which command the sympathy of every loyal American citizen, were exerted for the protection of our common country, and aided its triumph.

The town has thought fit to signify its honor for a few of its sons by raising an obelisk in the square. It is a simple pile enough, — a few slabs of granite, dug just below the surface of the soil, and laid upon the top of it; but as we have learned that the up-heaved mountain, from which these discs or flakes were broken, was once a glowing mass at white heat, slowly crystallized, then uplifted by the central fires of the globe: so the roots of the events it appropriately marks are in the heart of the universe. I shall say of this obelisk, planted here in our quiet plains, what Richter says of the volcano in the fair landscape of Naples: "Vesuvius stands in this poem of Nature, and exalts everything, as war does the age."

The art of the architect and the sense of the town have made these dumb stones speak; have, if I may borrow the old language of the church, converted these elements from a secular to a sacred and spiritual use; have made them look to the past and the future; have given them a meaning for the imagination and the heart. The sense of the town, the eloquent inscriptions the shaft now bears, the memories of these mar-

tyrs, the noble names which yet have gathered only their first fame, whatever good grows out of the war to the country, the largest results, the future power and genius of the land, will go on clothing this shaft with daily beauty and spiritual life. 'T is certain that a plain stone like this, standing on such memories, having no reference to utilities, but only to the grand instincts of the civil and moral man, mixes with surrounding nature,—by day, with the changing seasons,—by night, the stars roll over it gladly,—becomes a sentiment, a poet, a prophet, an orator, to every townsman and passenger, an altar where the noble youth shall in all time come to make his secret vows.

The old Monument, a short half-mile from this house, stands to signalize the first Revolution, where the people resisted offensive usurpations, offensive taxes of the British Parliament, claiming that there should be no tax without representation. Instructed by events, after the quarrel began, the Americans took higher ground, and stood for political independence. But, in the necessities of the hour, they overlooked the moral law, and winked at a practical exception to the Bill of Rights they had drawn up. They winked at the exception, believing it insignificant. But the moral law, the nature of things, did not wink at it, but kept its eye wide open. It turned out that this one violation was a subtle poison, which in eighty years

corrupted the whole overgrown body politic, and brought the alternative of extirpation of the poison or ruin to the Republic.

This new Monument is built to mark the arrival of the nation at the new principle, — say, rather, at its new acknowledgment, for the principle is as old as Heaven, — that only that State can live, in which injury to the least member is recognized as damage to the whole.

Reform must begin at home. The aim of the hour was to re-construct the South; but first the North had to be re-constructed. Its own theory and practice of liberty had got sadly out of gear, and must be corrected. It was done on the instant. A thunder-storm at sea sometimes reverses the magnets in the ship, and south is north. The storm of war works the like miracle on men. Every democrat who went South came back a republican, like the governors who, in Buchanan's time, went to Kansas, and instantly took the free-state colors. War, says the poet, is

"the arduous strife,
To which the triumph of all good is given."

Every principle is a war-note. When the rights of man are recited under any old government, every one of them is a declaration of war. War civilizes, re-arranges the population, distributing by ideas,—. the innovators on one side, the antiquaries on the

other. It opens the eyes wider. Once we were patriots up to the town-bounds, or the State-line. But when you replace the love of family or clan by a principle, as freedom, instantly that fire runs over the State-line into New Hampshire, Vermont, New York and Ohio, into the prairie and beyond, leaps the mountains, bridges river and lake, burns as hotly in Kansas and California as in Boston, and no chemist can discriminate between one soil and the other. It lifts every population to an equal power and merit.

As long as we debate in council, both sides may form their private guess what the event may be, or which is the strongest. But the moment you cry, "Every man to his tent, O Israel!" the delusions of hope and fear are at an end; — the strength is now to be tested by the eternal facts. There will be no doubt more. The world is equal to itself. The secret architecture of things begins to disclose itself; the fact that all things were made on a basis of right; that justice is really desired by all intelligent beings; that opposition to it is against the nature of things; and that, whatever may happen in this hour or that, the years and the centuries are always pulling down the wrong and building up the right.

The war made the Divine Providence credible to many who did not believe the good Heaven quite honest. Every man was an abolitionist by conviction,

but did not believe that his neighbor was. The opinions of masses of men, which the tactics of primary caucuses and the proverbial timidity of trade had concealed, the war discovered; and it was found, contrary to all popular belief, that the country was at heart abolitionist, and for the Union was ready to die.

As cities of men are the first effects of civilization, and also instantly causes of more civilization, so armies, which are only wandering cities, generate a vast heat, and lift the spirit of the soldiers who compose them to the boiling point. The armies mustered in the North were as much missionaries to the mind of the country, as they were carriers of material force, and had the vast advantage of carrying whither they marched a higher civilization. Of course, there are noble men everywhere, and there are such in the South; and the noble know the noble, wherever they meet; and we have all heard passages of generous and exceptional behavior exhibited by individuals there to our officers and men, during the war. But the common people, rich or poor, were the narrowest and most conceited of mankind, as arrogant as the negroes on the Gambia river; and, by the way, it looks as if the editors of the Southern press were in all times selected from this class. The invasion of Northern farmers, mechanics, engineers, tradesmen, lawyers and students did more than forty years of peace had done to educate

the South. "This will be a slow business," writes our Concord captain home, "for we have to stop and civilize the people as we go along."

It is an interesting part of the history, the manner in which this incongruous militia were made soldiers. That was done again on the Kansas plan. Our farmers went to Kansas as peaceable, God-fearing men as the members of our school-committee here. But when the Border raids were let loose on their villages, these people, who turned pale at home if called to dress a cut finger, on witnessing the butchery done by the Missouri riders on women and babes, were so beside themselves with rage, that they became on the instant the bravest soldiers and the most determined avengers. And the first events of the war of the Rebellion gave the like training to the new recruits.

All sorts of men went to the war, — the roughs, men who liked harsh play and violence, men for whom pleasure was not strong enough, but who wanted pain, and found sphere at last for their superabundant energy; then the adventurous type New-Englander, with his appetite for novelty and travel; the village politician, who could now verify his newspaper knowledge, see the South, and amass what a stock of adventures to retail hereafter at the fireside, or to the well-known companions on the mill-dam; young men, also, of excellent education and polished manners, delicately

brought up; mainly farmers, skilful mechanics, young tradesmen, men hitherto of narrow opportunities of knowing the world, but well taught in the grammar-schools. But perhaps in every one of these classes were idealists, men who went from a religious duty. I have a note of a conversation that occurred in our first company, the morning before the battle of Bull Run. At a halt in the march, a few of our boys were sitting on a rail fence talking together whether it was right to sacrifice themselves. One of them said, "he had been thinking a good deal about it, last night, and he thought one was never too young to die for a principle." One of our later volunteers, on the day when he left home, in reply to my question, How can you be spared from your farm, now that your father is so ill? said: "I go because I shall always be sorry if I did not go when the country called me. I can go as well as another." One wrote to his father these words: — "You may think it strange that I, who have always naturally rather shrunk from danger, should wish to enter the army; but there is a higher Power that tunes the hearts of men, and enables them to see their duty, and gives them courage to face the dangers with which those duties are attended." And the captain writes home of another of his men, — "B—— comes from a sense of duty and love of country, and these are the soldiers you can depend upon."

None of us can have forgotten how sharp a test to try our peaceful people with, was the first call for troops. I doubt not many of our soldiers could repeat the confession of a youth whom I knew in the beginning of the war, who enlisted in New York, went to the field, and died early. Before his departure he confided to his sister that he was naturally a coward, but was determined that no one should ever find it out; that he had long trained himself by forcing himself, on the suspicion of any near danger, to go directly up to it, cost him what struggles it might. Yet it is from this temperament of sensibility that great heroes have been formed.

Our first company was led by an officer who had grown up in this village from a boy. The older among us can well remember him at school, at play and at work, all the way up, the most amiable, sensible, unpretending of men; fair, blonde, the rose lived long in his cheek; grave, but social, and one of the last men in this town you would have picked out for the rough dealing of war, — not a trace of fierceness, much less of recklessness, or of the devouring thirst for excitement; tender as a woman in his care for a cough or a chilblain in his men; had troches and arnica in his pocket for them. The army officers were welcome to their jest on him as too kind for a captain, and later, as the colonel who got off his horse, when he saw one of

his men limp on the march, and told him to ride. But *he* knew that his men had found out, first that he was captain, then that he was colonel, and neither dared nor wished to disobey him. He was a man without conceit, who never fancied himself a philosopher or a saint; the most modest and amiable of men, engaged in common duties, but equal always to the occasion; and the war showed him still equal, however stern and terrible the occasion grew, — disclosed in him a strong good sense, great fertility of resource, the helping hand, and then the moral qualities of a commander, — a patience not to be tired out, a serious devotion to the cause of the country that never swerved, a hope that never failed. He was a puritan in the army, with traits that remind one of John Brown, — an integrity incorruptible, and an ability that always rose to the need.

You will remember that these colonels, captains and lieutenants, and the privates too, are domestic men just wrenched away from their families and their business, by this rally of all the manhood in the land. They have notes to pay at home ; have farms, shops, factories, affairs of every kind, to think of, and write home about. Consider what sacrifice and havoc in business arrangements this war-blast made. They have to think carefully of every last resource at home, on which their wives or mothers may fall back ; upon the

little account in the savings-bank, the grass that can be sold, the old cow, or the heifer. These necessities make the topics of the ten thousand letters with which the mail-bags came loaded day by day. These letters play a great part in the war. The writing of letters made the Sunday in every camp;—meantime they are without the means of writing. After the first marches, there is no letter-paper, there are no envelopes, no postage-stamps, for these were wetted into a solid mass in the rains and mud. Some of these letters are written on the back of old bills, some on brown paper, or strips of newspaper; written by firelight, making the short night shorter; written on the knee, in the mud, with pencil, six words at a time; or in the saddle, and have to stop because the horse will not stand still. But the words are proud and tender, — "Tell mother I will not disgrace her"; "tell her not to worry about me, for I know she would not have had me stay at home if she could as well as not." The letters of the captain are the dearest treasures of this town. Always devoted, sometimes anxious, sometimes full of joy at the deportment of his comrades, they contain the sincere praise of men whom I now see in this assembly. If Marshal Monthic's Memoirs are the Bible of soldiers, as Henry IV. of France said, Colonel Prescott might furnish the Book of Epistles.

He writes, "You do n't know how one gets attached to a company by living with them and sleeping with them all the time. I know every man by heart. I know every man's weak spot, — who is shaky, and who is true blue." He never remits his care of the men, aiming to hold them to their good habits and to keep them cheerful. For the first point, he keeps up a constant acquaintance with them; urges their correspondence with their friends; writes news of them home, urging his own correspondent to visit their families and keep them informed about the men; encourages a temperance society which is formed in the camp. "I have not had a man drunk, or affected by liquor, since we came here." At one time, he finds his company unfortunate in having fallen between two companies of quite another class, — 't is profanity all the time. Yet instead of a bad influence on our men thinks it works the other way, — it disgusts them.

One day he writes: "I expect to have a time, this forenoon, with the officer from West Point who drills us. He is very profane, and I will not stand it. If he does not stop it, I shall march my men right away when he is drilling them. There is a fine for officers swearing in the army, and I have too many young men that are not used to such talk. I told the colonel this morning I should do it, and shall, — do n't care what the consequence is. This lieutenant seems to think that these men who never saw a gun, can drill as well

as he, who has been at West Point four years." At night he adds: "I told that officer from West Point, this morning, that he could not swear at my company as he did yesterday; told him I would not stand it any way. I told him I had a good many young men in my company, whose mothers asked me to look after them, and I should do so, and not allow them to hear such language, especially from an officer whose duty it was to set them a better example. Told him I did not swear myself, and would not allow him to. He looked at me as much as to say, *Do you know whom you are talking to?* and I looked at him as much as to say, *Yes, I do.* He looked rather ashamed, but went through the drill without an oath." So much for the care of their morals. His next point is to keep them cheerful. 'T is better than medicine. He has games of base ball, and pitching quoits, and euchre, whilst part of the military discipline is sham-fights.

The best men heartily second him, and invent excellent means of their own. When, afterwards, five of these men were prisoners in the Parish Prison in New Orleans, they set themselves to use the time to the wisest advantage, — formed a debating club, wrote a daily or weekly newspaper, called it "Stars and Stripes." It advertises, "prayer meeting at 7 o'clock, in cell No. 8, second floor," and their own printed record is a proud and affecting narrative.

Whilst the regiment was encamped at Camp Andrew, near Alexandria, in June, 1861, marching orders came. Colonel Lawrence sent for eight wagons, but only three came. On these they loaded all the canvas of the tents, but took no tent-poles. "It looked very much like a severe thunder-storm," writes the captain, "and I knew the men would all have to sleep out of doors, unless we carried them. So I took six poles, and went to the colonel, and told him I had got the poles for two tents, which would cover twenty-four men, and unless he ordered me not to carry them, I should do so. He said he had no objection, only thought they would be too much for me. We only had about twelve men," (the rest of the company being, perhaps, on picket or other duty,) "and some of them have their heavy knapsacks and guns to carry, so could not carry any poles. We started and marched two miles without stopping to rest, not having had anything to eat, and being very hot and dry." At this time Captain Prescott was daily threatened with sickness, and suffered the more from this heat. "I told Lieutenant Bowers, this morning, that I could afford to be sick from bringing the tent-poles, for it saved the whole regiment from sleeping out doors; for they would not have thought of it, if I had not taken mine. The major had tried to discourage me; — said, 'perhaps, if I carried them over, some other company would get them'; — told him, per-

haps he did not think I was smart." He had the satisfaction to see the whole regiment enjoying the protection of these tents.

In the disastrous battle of Bull Run, this company behaved well, and the regimental officers believed, what is now the general conviction of the country, that the misfortunes of the day were not so much owing to the fault of the troops, as to the insufficiency of the combinations by the general officers. It happened, also, that the Fifth Massachusetts was almost unofficered. The colonel was, early in the day, disabled by a casualty; the lieut.-colonel, the major and the adjutant were already transferred to new regiments, and their places were not yet filled. The three months of the enlistment expired a few days after the battle.

In the fall of 1861, the old Artillery company of this town was re-organized, and Captain Richard Barrett received a commission in March, 1862, from the State, as its commander. This company, chiefly recruited here, was later embodied in the Forty-seventh Regiment, Massachusetts Volunteers, enlisted as nine months' men, and sent to New Orleans, where they were employed in guard duty during their term of service. Captain Humphrey H. Buttrick, lieutenant in this regiment, as he had been already lieutenant in Captain Prescott's company in 1861, went out again in August, 1864, a captain in the Fifty-ninth Massachu-

setts, and saw hard service in the Ninth Corps, under General Burnside. The regiment being formed of veterans, and in fields requiring great activity and exposure, suffered extraordinary losses, Captain Buttrick and one other officer being the only officers in it who were neither killed, wounded nor captured. In August, 1862, on the new requisition for troops, when it was becoming difficult to meet the draft, — mainly through the personal example and influence of Mr. Sylvester Lovejoy, twelve men, including himself, were enlisted for three years, and, being soon after enrolled in the Fortieth Massachusetts, went to the war; and a very good account has been heard, not only of the regiment, but of the talents and virtues of these men.

After the return of the three months' company to Concord, in 1861, Captain Prescott raised a new company of volunteers, and Captain Bowers another. Each of these companies included recruits from this town, and they formed part of the Thirty-second Regiment of Massachusetts Volunteers. Enlisting for three years, and remaining to the end of the war, these troops saw every variety of hard service which the war offered, and, though suffering at first some disadvantage from change of commanders, and from severe losses, they grew at last, under the command of Colonel Prescott, to an excellent reputation, attested by the names of the thirty battles they were authorized to

inscribe on their flag, and by the important position usually assigned them in the field.

I have found many notes of their rough experience in the march and in the field. In McClellan's retreat in the Peninsula, in July, 1862, " it is all our men can do to draw their feet out of the mud. We marched one mile through mud, without exaggeration, one foot deep. — a good deal of the way over my boots, and with short rations; on one day nothing but liver, blackberries, and pennyroyal tea." — "At Fredericksburg we lay eleven hours in one spot without moving, except to rise and fire." The next note is, " cracker for a day and a half, — but all right." Another day, "had not left the ranks for thirty hours, and the nights were broken by frequent alarms. How would Concord people," he asks, " like to pass the night on the battlefield, and hear the dying cry for help, and not be able to go to them?" But the regiment did good service at Harrison's Landing, and at Antietam, under Colonel Parker; and at Fredericksburg, in December, Lieutenant-Colonel Prescott loudly expresses his satisfaction at his comrades, now and then particularizing names: " Bowers, Shepard and Lauriat are as brave as lions."

At the battle of Gettysburg, in July, 1863, the brigade of which the Thirty-second Regiment formed a part was in line of battle seventy-two hours, and

suffered severely. Colonel Prescott's regiment went in with two hundred and ten men, nineteen officers. On the second of July they had to cross the famous wheat field, under fire from the rebels in front and on both flanks. Seventy men were killed or wounded out of seven companies. Here Francis Buttrick, whose manly beauty all of us remember, and Sergeant Appleton, an excellent soldier, were fatally wounded. The colonel was hit by three bullets. "I feel," he writes, "I have much to be thankful for that my life is spared, although I would willingly die to have the regiment do as well as they have done. Our colors had several holes made, and were badly torn. One bullet hit the staff which the bearer had in his hand. The color-bearer is brave as a lion; he will go anywhere you say, and no questions asked; his name is Marshall Davis." The colonel took evident pleasure in the fact that he could account for all his men. There were so many killed, so many wounded, — but no missing. For that word "missing" was apt to mean skulking. Another incident: "A friend of Lieutenant Barrow complains that we did not treat his body with respect, inasmuch as we did not send it home. I think we were very fortunate to save it at all, for in ten minutes after he was killed the rebels occupied the ground, and we had to carry him and all of our wounded nearly two miles in blankets. There was no place nearer than Baltimore where we

could have got a coffin, and I suppose it was eighty miles there. We laid him in two double blankets, and then sent off a long distance and got boards off a barn to make the best coffin we could, and gave him burial."

After Gettysburg, Colonel Prescott remarks that our regiment is highly complimented. When Colonel Gurney, of the Ninth, came to him the next day to tell him that "folks are just beginning to appreciate the Thirty-second Regiment: it always was a good regiment, and people are just beginning to find it out"; Colonel Prescott notes in his journal, — "Pity they have not found it out before it was all gone. We have a hundred and seventy-seven guns this morning."

Let me add an extract from the official report of the brigade commander: "Word was sent by General Barnes that, when we retired, we should fall back under cover of the woods. This order was communicated to Colonel Prescott, whose regiment was then under the hottest fire. Understanding it to be a peremptory order to retire them, he replied, 'I do n't want to retire; I am not ready to retire; I can hold this place'; and he made good his assertion. Being informed that he misunderstood the order, which was only to inform him how to retire when it became necessary, he was satisfied, and he and his command held their ground manfully." It was said that Colonel

Prescott's reply, when reported, pleased the Acting Brigadier-General Sweitzer mightily.

After Gettysburg, the Thirty-second Regiment saw hard service at Rappahannock Station; and at Baltimore, in Virginia, where they were drawn up in battle order for ten days successively: crossing the Rapidan, and suffering from such extreme cold, a few days later, at Mine Run, that the men were compelled to break rank and run in circles to keep themselves from being frozen. On the third of December, they went into winter quarters.

I must not follow the multiplied details that make the hard work of the next year. But the campaign in the Wilderness surpassed all their worst experience hitherto of the soldier's life. On the third of May, they crossed the Rapidan for the fifth time. On the twelfth, at Laurel Hill, the regiment had twenty-one killed and seventy-five wounded, including five officers. "The regiment has been in the front and centre since the battle begun, eight and a half days ago, and is now building breastworks on the Fredericksburg road. This has been the hardest fight the world ever knew. I think the loss of our army will be forty thousand. Every day, for the last eight days, there has been a terrible battle the whole length of the line. One day they drove us; but it has been regular bull-dog fighting." On the twenty-first, they had been, for seventeen

days and nights, under arms without rest. On the twenty-third, they crossed the North Anna, and achieved a great success. On the thirtieth, we learn, "Our regiment has never been in the second line since we crossed the Rapidan, on the third." On the night of the thirtieth, — "The hardest day we ever had. We have been in the first line twenty-six days, and fighting every day but two; whilst your newspapers talk of the inactivity of the Army of the Potomac. If those writers could be here and fight all day, and sleep in the trenches, and be called up several times in the night by picket-firing, they would not call it inactive." June fourth is marked in the diary as "An awful day; — two hundred men lost to the command"; and not until the fifth of June comes at last a respite for a short space, during which the men drew shoes and socks, and the officers were able to send to the wagons and procure a change of clothes, for the first time in five weeks.

But from these incessant labors there was now to be rest for one head, — the honored and beloved commander of the regiment. On the sixteenth of June, they crossed the James River, and marched to within three miles of Petersburg. Early in the morning of the eighteenth they went to the front, formed line of battle, and were ordered to take the Norfolk and Petersburg Railroad from the Rebels. In this charge,

Colonel George L. Prescott was mortally wounded. After driving the enemy from the railroad, crossing it, and climbing the farther bank to continue the charge, he was struck in front of his command by a musket ball, which entered his breast near the heart. He was carried off the field to the division hospital, and died on the following morning. On his death-bed, he received the needless assurances of his general, that "he had done more than all his duty," — needless to a conscience so faithful and unspotted. One of his townsmen and comrades, a sergeant in his regiment, writing to his own family, uses these words: "He was one of the few men who fight for principle. He did not fight for glory, honor nor money, but because he thought it his duty. These are not my feelings only, but of the whole regiment."

On the first of January, 1865, the Thirty-second Regiment made itself comfortable in log huts, a mile south of our rear line of works before Petersburg. On the fourth of February, sudden orders came to move next morning at daylight. At Dabney's Mills, in a sharp fight, they lost seventy-four in killed, wounded and missing. Here Major Shepard was taken prisoner. The lines were held until the tenth, with more than usual suffering from snow and hail and intense cold, added to the annoyance of the artillery fire. On the first of April, the regiment connected with Sheridan's

cavalry, near the Five Forks, and took important part in that battle which opened Petersburg and Richmond, and forced the surrender of Lee. On the ninth, they marched in support of the cavalry, and were advancing in a grand charge, when the white flag of General Lee appeared. The brigade of which the Thiry-second Regiment formed part was detailed to receive the formal surrender of the Rebel arms. The homeward march begun on the thirteenth, and the regiment was mustered out in the field, at Washington, on the twenty-eighth of June, and arrived in Boston on the first of July.

Fellow-citizens: The obelisk records only the names of the dead. There is something partial in this distribution of honor. Those who went through those dreadful fields and returned not, deserve much more than all the honor we can pay. But those also who went through the same fields and returned alive, put just as much at hazard as those who died, and, in other countries, would wear distinctive badges of honor as long as they lived. I hope the disuse of such medals or badges in this country only signifies that everybody knows these men, and carries their deed in such lively remembrance that they require no badge or reminder. I am sure I need not bespeak your gratitude to these fellow-citizens and neighbors of ours. I hope they will be content with the laurels of one war.

But let me, in behalf of this assembly, speak directly to you, our defenders, and say, that it is easy to see that if danger should ever threaten the homes which you guard, the knowledge of your presence will be a wall of fire for their protection. Brave men! you will hardly be called to see again fields as terrible as those you have already trampled with your victories.

There are people who can hardly read the names on yonder bronze tablet, the mist so gathers in their eyes. Three of the names are of sons of one family. A gloom gathers on this assembly, composed as it is of kindred men and women, for, in many houses, the dearest and noblest is gone from their hearthstone. Yet it is tinged with light from heaven. A duty so severe has been discharged, and with such immense results of good, lifting private sacrifice to the sublime, that, though the cannon volleys have a sound of funeral echoes, they can yet hear through them the benedictions of their country and mankind.

APPENDIX.

In the above Address I have been compelled to suppress more details of personal interest than I have used. But I do not like to omit the testimony to the character of the Commander of the Thirty-second Massachusetts Regiment, given in the following letter, by one of his soldiers:

NEAR PETERSBURG, VIRGINIA,
JUNE 20TH, 1864.

DEAR FATHER:

With feelings of deep regret, I inform you that Colonel Prescott, our brave and lamented leader, is no more. He was shot through the body, near the heart, on the eighteenth day of June, and died the following morning. On the morning of the eighteenth, our division was not in line. Reveille was at an early hour, and before long we were moving to the front. Soon we passed the ground where the Ninth Corps drove the enemy from their fortified lines, and came upon and formed our line in rear of Crawford's Division. In front of us, and one mile distant, the Rebels' lines of works could be seen. Between us and them, and in a deep gulley, was the Norfolk and Petersburg Railroad. Soon the order came for us to take the railroad from the enemy, whose advance then held it. Four regiments of our brigade were to head the charge; so the 32nd Massachusetts, 62nd, 91st and 155th Pennsylvania regiments, under command of Colonel Gregory, moved forward in good order, the enemy keeping up a steady fire all the time. All went well till we reached the road. The Rebels left when they saw us advance, and, when we reached the road, they were running away. But here our troubles

began. The banks, on each side of the road, were about thirty feet high, and, being stiff clay, were nearly perpendicular. We got down well enough, because we got started, and were rolled to the bottom, a confused pile of Yanks. Now to climb the other side! It was impossible to get up by climbing, for the side of it was like the side of a house. By dint of getting on each others' shoulders, and making holes for our feet with bayonets, a few of us got up; reaching our guns down to the others, we all finally got over. Meanwhile, a storm of bullets was rained upon us. Through it all, Colonel Prescott was cool and collected, encouraging the men to do their best. After we were almost all across, he moved out in front of the line, and called the men out to him, saying, "Come on men; form our line here." The colorbearer stepped towards him, when a bullet struck the Colonel, passed through him; and wounded the color-bearer, Sergeant Giles, of Company G. Calmly the Colonel turned, and said, "I am wounded; some one help me off." A sergeant of Company B, and one of the 21st Pennsylvania, helped him off. This man told me, last night, all that the Colonel said, while going off. He was afraid we would be driven back, and wanted these men to stick by him. He said, "I die for my country." He seemed to be conscious that death was near to him, and said the wound was near his heart; wanted the sergeant of Company B, to write to his family, and tell them all about him. He will write to Mrs. Prescott, probably; but if they do not hear from some one an account of his death, I wish you would show this to Mrs. Prescott. He died in the division hospital, night before last, and his remains will probably be sent to Concord. We lament his loss in the regiment very much. He was like a father to us,—always counselling us to be firm in the path of duty, and setting the example himself. I think a more moral man, or one more likely to enter the kingdom of heaven, cannot be found in the Army of the Potomac. No man ever heard him swear, or saw him use liquor, since we were in the service. I wish there was some way for the regiment to pay some tribute to his memory.

But the folks at home must do this, for the present. The Thirty-second Regiment has lost its leader, and calls on the people of Concord to console the afflicted family of the brave departed, by showing their esteem for him in some manner. He was one of the few men who fight for principle,—pure principle. He did not fight for glory, honor nor money, but because he thought it his duty. These are not my feelings only, but of the whole regiment. I want you to show this to every one, so they can see what we thought of the Colonel, and how he died in front of his regiment. God bless and comfort his poor family. Perhaps people think soldiers have no feeling, but it is not so. We feel deep anxiety for the families of all our dear comrades.

CHARLES BARTLETT,
Sergeant Company G,
Thirty-second Massachusetts Volunteers.

POEM,
By F. B. Sanborn.

Slow gliding hours to these broad meadows bring
Spring's humid fragrance and the flowers of spring;
Bluebird and robin on the branches sway,
Of silvered willow and of maple gay,
That faintly glimmer mid the sunny haze
And petulant pelting rain of April days;
Sweet is their song, sweeter the season new,
When lands again are green and waters blue.

As these light troubadours of air return,
While elm-trees tassel and the maples burn,
Still in the midst of their exulting strain
The ear that hearkens notes a sad refrain;
Whate'er the season lavishes of bliss,
Some sorrow pains them, some past joy they miss.
"Can human hearts," you cry, "sink in despair
When spring's bright pennons rustle in the air?"
Nay, but can men the mournful past forget,
When merle and sparrow are not happy yet?

Let us remember, — let the tale be told
How o'er the land war's sudden tempest rolled,
How year by year the doubtful battle raged,.
Till peace was earned and Heaven's just wrath assuaged:
Yet, as the angry clouds asunder broke,
The sullen thunder launched a final stroke,

That smote our guiltless leader in his hour
Of most secure and least vindictive power.
Bloodily closed what bloodily began
With slaughter of that far-foreseeing man,
Whose spirit, from the scaffold where he died,
Armies and senates could inspire and guide.

Between these two — the first and latest slain —
How many martyrs did our annals gain!
Each hamlet — nay, each household in the land
Added some member to the heroic band.
The grief they left, the glory they achieved,
Touches all hearts, for all have been bereaved:
And we can share the triumph and the pain
Of all that dwell in our unshorn domain.
Yet, though to all is due the same great debt,
Our own dead champions claim more just regret;
And these we honor, not with words alone,
Nor transient forms of perishable stone,
But here their all-outlasting shaft shall stand,
Hewn from the core primeval of the land.

What memories shall you sculptured names recall!
Read when the sunlight on the lines shall fall,
Or when the moon, late comrade of their camp,
Lends the soft lustre of her friendly lamp;
Or some great star, the sentry's eye that caught
And guided homeward all his midnight thought,
Year upon year shall trace with twinkling flame
The bronzed letters of his buried name.

SOLDIERS' MONUMENT.

The young shall listen while the old men tell
The deeds of these that earned renown so well;
Shall hear how Sumter saw our flag, unfurled
Amid the smoke of battle round it curled,
Give to the eye of heaven its stars, as fair
As any nightly glories clustering there;
How, when the traitor's cannon stained those charms,
With sudden wrath the nation sprang to arms.
Thousands on thousands thronged, — abandoned now
The desk, the loom, the anvil, and the plow.
Navies betrayed and blazing on the shore
Lighted them on through howling Baltimore,
Till round the threatened Capitol they drew
The lines long tried but never broken through.

'T was war's first stanza; — but the strain was long,
And swift the changes of the fearful song.
The eager onset, the dismayed retreat,
The loitering army, the victorious fleet,
The baffled leaders, the slow-gathering might
Of peaceful millions arming for the fight,
The circle narrowing round the desperate foe,
The fatal marches and the conquering blow;
This shall the village chronicler rehearse,
And set these names in order through his verse.
"Here *Prescott* led the charge, — this fort he scaled,
And here laid down the life so oft assailed;
Such swift release to *Ripley* was denied,
Venturous in fight, yet not in fight he died;
Buttrick, that fought the British at the Bridge,
Fought in his sons on Gettysburg's long ridge."

So shall he say, and none of all forget
Whose grateful tablet in this stone is set;
Nor less commemorate, though with less lament,
The brave survivors of each regiment.

Close clings Tradition to New England mould,
She haunts the fireside of the homestead old,
Roams moss-grown pastures where the school-boys go,
And chats with mowers in the meadows low;
But she, like all things mortal, must decay;
And when her voice has vanished quite away,
The future age, of ours oblivious grown,
Shall question History and this mindful stone;
Shall ask for what these fought, what good was won
By all this marching and campaigning done.
Then shall the Muse of this long-buried age
Lay wide her volume at the proudest page;
No more she'll quote the records of the dead,
Nor twine her laurels for a leader's head,
Nor this man great nor that man wise she'll call.
"GOD and the PEOPLE so directed all,
That, from the foulest stains of former shame,
A noble nation then retrieved her name;
Ascending justly from that fortunate hour
Thou seest her at the topmost height of power.
These were her sons, — their names the years have spared,
Her woes they suffered and her victory shared;
Myriads like these, nor baser nor more brave,
Have slept unnoticed in their nameless grave.
Whatever since of good this nation sees,
She owes it all to humble sons like these."

REMARKS,

By Hon. George S. Boutwell.

My Friends:

I feel that it is entirely inappropriate for me to mingle in what must be considered funereal solemnities; yet, on your part, it is just to yourselves and to posterity, seeking the aid of such memorials as wealth and art can furnish, to preserve the names and worth of those of your fellow-citizens who fell in the war for the preservation of the Union.

These memorials, though designed for one or for a few, are yet in fact a tribute to many, — to all. So gigantic was the Rebellion, so vast was the theatre of the war, and so great the number of persons engaged in it, that the services of individuals, even of those most distinguished, were comparatively unimportant in securing the great result. The country was saved by the energy, the courage, the worth, the patriotism, the statesmanlike forethought of the great mass of the people. Local history and tradition will bear to other times the names of the great number of persons who took part in the contest; general history and a more public fame will notice the distinguished few; but, after all, the fact will remain that our triumph was due

to an exalted, marvellous exhibition of popular power. The events of the war teach and prove that this government is at once the wisest and strongest of human governments, and that its wisdom and strength proceed from the great body of the people. It would be a sorrow without relief, as we remember the honored dead, — we should look upon the future of our country without hope, if, after all our sacrifices, the nation had failed in its efforts to re-establish the government upon the unchanging principles of justice. If human progress can ever be adequate compensation for the destruction of human life, we may even now, in this presence, look complacently upon the great sacrifice the nation has made, as we survey the future in the dawning light of a better day for our country and for the whole human race.

REMARKS,

By Wm. Schouler, Esq.

LADIES AND GENTLEMEN:

I am so unused to speaking that I hardly know how to express myself on this occasion, it is so long since I have addressed any considerable body of men; but I could not resist the temptation of complying with the invitation to come to Old Concord to be present at the dedication of the Monument. The associations of my early life are kindly connected with this town, and I am glad always to come here.

The services of to-day have been of peculiar and unspeakable interest to me. It was my fortune to know Colonel Prescott, and many of the men whose names I find inscribed upon the tablet of that Monument. I know that they were good men. I know that there has been nothing said here by their fellow-citizens but what was true. I have no doubt at all that the real history of Massachusetts, the real feeling of the people, the true sympathies and inward promptings of the heart, can better be ascertained by the correspondence which came from the army, and which was so eloquently and appropriately alluded to by Mr. Emerson. During the war, while I was the Adjutant-General of the Common-

wealth, every regiment and every company and every officer, and, I was going to say, almost every man, in some way or other, I had something to do with. During the five years of the war, to show that our men knew how to read and write, I received myself from the army and from the families of our men over twenty thousand letters. They are every one of them safely filed away in the office of the Adjutant-General; and I wrote in answer to them, and on other matters, over twenty-five thousand letters. The correspondence of the Governor was even greater than that of the Adjutant-General.

I am now engaged, and have been, evenings and afternoons, for some weeks, in looking over the correspondence of the executive department, to make extracts and notes for the purpose of using them in writing a history of Massachusetts in the war; and I am certain that no community on the face of the earth can show a record and correspondence so full of interest as can be shown, and as is now on file in the department of the State of Massachusetts.

Our boys were good boys. They were brave men. They went to fight, as Judge Hoar and Mr. Emerson have so well said, for their rights, and they knew their rights, — they knew what they were fighting for. They did not go there with their hearts full of hatred. Six years ago to-day, and almost at this very hour, our

Sixth Regiment was attacked in the streets of Baltimore, and the first blood was shed in defence of the American Union as it was, on the same day, in 1775, in Concord, for liberty and independence. And of these men who went from Massachusetts to defend the capital, with their haversacks and knapsacks and muskets, there was not one that would not have divided his meat in his haversack with any southern man, if he had been Union or even Rebel, if he had been a prisoner or was in trouble.

Our men were good Christian men. Their record is the treasure of the State and country; and I am glad, for one, that in this old and historic town, there should be another monument erected to commemorate the sufferings and sacrifices of your soldiers and the noble, generous, and brave Prescott, who fell in Virginia, but whose body now is interred in your cemetery beneath the pines and the trees he loved so well.

Ladies and gentlemen: I thank you for listening to the few remarks I have made, but, after the great intellectual treat we have listened to, I shall not certainly occupy more of your time.

REMARKS,

By Colonel Parker.

Mr. President and Fellow-Citizens:

To-day, throughout the Christian world, before tens of thousands of holy altars, Christian men are bowed in sackcloth and ashes, in contemplation of that mysterious sacrifice, "once offered for us all," the expiation for the sins of the whole world.

Two years ago this Good Friday, the chief of our nation sealed with his blood and life the book of our civil war; and the name of him, who, by his conservative good sense and homely humor, had come to be the beloved of the people, was enrolled among those of the patriot martyrs.

Ninety-two years ago this April day, the yeomen of this county of Middlesex — your ancestors and my ancestors — initiated upon this very soil the war of Independence, and made the raid of the foe to become a race for his cantonments. Since then, at least, Massachusetts does not breed traitors. The blood of your people, shed that day, has proved the nourishment of patriotism and the blight of treason. The veil of the future we cannot raise, but we may be sure that whatever may come hereafter, there shall always be upon

old Middlesex soil, within the limits of Old Concord, minute-men like them of '75 and '61, who will defend their country's flag, their country's honor and the name of their ancestry.

Here then, not unfittingly, we are assembled with oratory and music, with ode and lyric, and with prayer and praise to God, to dedicate this obelisk, raised to the memory of the latest generation of the patriot soldiers of Old Concord town, who, genuine descendants of them who became rebels for the sake of independence, have died that the autonomy, won by the struggle of their fathers, might be transmitted to their children; — that the nationality once wrested from external rule might be maintained against internal rebellion.

Here we give due honor to your quota of that " noble army of martyrs," of which President Lincoln was the most illustrious and the last. Their and your examples are not yet fruited forever; but yonder lads, whose voices, joyous at their games, ring like holiday music to our ears, may yet take up the honorable burden of their fathers, — the flag of their country, — and defend it yet again with *their* fortunes and *their* lives.

Here, remembering the solemnity of this holiest day of the holy week, and the sacrifice which it commemorates, we bear in mind and heart your sacred dead as men " not lost but gone before," (an honorable prece-

dence in the procession of immortality;) not hopeless of what shall be, but looking to Him, our Lord Jesus, who is the Resurrection and the Life.

Not unfitting, then, is the purpose to the day, or the day to its purpose.

To me, as I read the names inscribed on yonder bronze, there appear not merely names but the faces of my comrades, and the forms of my soldiers; the stalwart colonel, who fell in the very shadow of his colors, amid the roar of battle, and the cheers of a successful charge; the quiet boy corporal, fair in face, gentle in demeanor, exact in duty, who breathed his life away in the malaria of those pestilential swamps, less fortunate than they who met death at the hand of the foe, but dying none the less for his country and for you; — faces and forms that I have seen in every vicissitude of soldier life, and which can never be dead to me.

You have done well, citizens of Concord, to honor your fallen braves, and to-day to crown you shalt with your laurels. Let it stand through coming time, to be an incentive to them who come after us, and that from it they may know that it is honorable to die for one's country. But forget not, I pray you, them who remain, and who, in an equal spirit of patriotic devotion, dared, but escaped, the fate of these your soldier dead. Let not your sense of obligation be crystallized in these stones, like them to monumental and

cold; give to the veterans the warm corner at your firesides and the preference in your patronage; let them tell — even if for the hundredth time, let them recite, and to the end, the story of their battle life. They have earned this indulgence at your hands. But for them, and these their dead compatriots, — but for their weary marches, their frequent hunger, their constant exposure, their sickness, wounds or death, what would your country be to-day? — the spoil and the sport of the old-world nations; she who *is* their lord and arbiter.

REMARKS,

By Colonel Lucius B. Marsh.

Ladies and Gentlemen:

I do n't feel that I have hardly a right to speak to you on this occasion. It is a family gathering. And yet I do remember, with grateful feelings, that this good town of Concord gave me that excellent company that always stood at the right of my regiment. We have heard to-day, most eloquently, the history and writings of those that are dead. And I can say most truly of that first company, that the sainted dead Colonel Prescott commanded — which went out in the fifth regiment, and was the company which was afterwards commanded by Captain Richard Barrett, in the forty-seventh regiment, and which has to-day presented itself to us — that every peculiarity which marked the character of its men was a constant weight upon their captain's mind; that he looked after every want; that he looked after everything which should characterize them as young men growing up into life; and that, having left fathers, mothers, children and wives at home, they should preserve that character while abroad. I say all this and every other virtue clustered round and pervaded always the character of Captain Barrett, who

now and then commanded this company. And I say to you, my friends of Concord, that when you gave me your sons, and, as it seems to-day, almost the last young man from the town, to fill that company, I said to you, "I will take good care of them." The captain of that company and his officers did take good care of them, and, in the providence of God, brought them — almost all, I think — back again to their homes. They went away good young men; they returned doubly good, for they had stood the temptations of the camp and came home tried and not found wanting in moral principle.

The remarks we have listened to this afternoon are weighty and are interesting. They tell us — O, how dearly they tell us, of those who left home and loved ones and all that were dear, and for the love of their country they left all these and went away to live in the field, in the swamps, or to die upon the battle-field. And now, gathered in this presence, having been requested to answer for the regiment of which one of the companies belonging to it came from this town principally, I would say that I tender to you, every one of you here in Concord and in this vicinity, who gave me their sons and brothers and their husbands, my sincere and warmest thanks for everything that was done while absent in the field, and for the care and kindness and attention that you paid them when they returned to their homes.

POEM,

By Sampson Mason.

Here, on the soil where freemen first
   Opposed our country's foes;
Here, where Oppression's chains were burst,
   Where smoke of conflict rose;

Here, where our fathers anxious met,
   On that bright April morn,
And fired the gun that echoes yet,
   Announcing Freedom born;

Here, now, to-day, we gather round,
   By inspiration led,
And rear upon this classic ground
   A mausoleum to the dead.

The martyrs of that gallant band,
   Who left this rural town,
When dire rebellion shook the land,
   To put rebellion down;

They left the peaceful walks of life,
   Homes, and the joys they yield,
For scenes of carnage, war, and strife,
   Death, and the battle-field.

With love of Liberty inspired,
  They knelt before her shrine;
A loyal zeal their bosoms fired; —
  "Our country, we are thine."

They are a nation's boast and pride,
  Who, at their country's call,
Have bravely fought, or nobly died,
  And gave their lives, — their all.

A nation's gratitude is theirs;
  It swells our hearts to-day;
Thus would we tell it to our heirs,
  When we have passed away.

Then rise, memorial to the brave,
  Their memories consecrate,
Who left their homes our homes to save,
  But met a soldier's fate.

Rise in thy modest grandeur; rise
  By patriotism reared;
This ancient town about thee lies,
  Historically revered.

What countless footsteps here will pause,
  And loiter at this shrine,
And mothers lead their orphan ones
  To spell a father's line.

The traveller, as he passes by,
  Upon it turns to gaze;
From base to apex lifts his eye,
  And thinks of battle days.

Oft shall the aged soldier here
  Linger round this spot,
Uttering, as his steps draw near,
  "Comrades, we're not forgot!"

Old Concord — patriotic town —
  Lets not her heroes sleep
Unmindful of their just renown,
  But green their memories keep.

The shaft that stands on yonder shore,
  Where flows Musketaquid,
Records our fathers' deeds of yore;
  This, what their children did.

Twin-like they rise, alike their aim,
  Both pointing to the sky;
Both sculptured o'er with deeds of fame,
  And names that cannot die.

Far down the vale of distant years
  Their shadows may they cast,
While morning throws his early beams,
  Or evening sheds her last.

That generations yet to be,
　These structures may behold,
And prize the boon of Liberty
　Above legacies of gold.

Thus shall the flame, enkindled here
　In seventeen seventy-five,
Illumine the whole hemisphere,
　And still be kept alive.

No foreign foe invade the shore,
　No civil broils within;
Sweet, smiling peace instead of war,
　Righteousness for sin.

Then shall the land indeed be blest;
　The stars and stripes shall wave;
No North, no South, no East, no West,
　No rebel and no slave.

www.ingramcontent.com/pod-product-compliance
Lightning Source LLC
Chambersburg PA
CBHW030352170426
43202CB00010B/1349